Fleeting Heart

A Collection of Poetry

By:

Megan Benjamin Evans

Fleeting Heart First Edition Copyright © 2014 By: Megan Benjamin Evans.

Editor: Dee Maurer

Cover Art: Megan Benjamin Evans

ISBN-13: 978-0990765219

ISBN-10: 0990765210

Credits & Acknowledgments

Words cannot express my gratitude to my friends John and Erica Pek for your generosity and being there in my great time of need. You both rock!

To Becket for his professional advice, assistance and friendship through this process. Not to mention the brilliant words he writes in poetic form that helps keep me going through the inevitable rough patches in life.

Last but not least I would like to thank my husband John and daughter Auriel. This book would not have been possible without your encouragement and putting up with my flights of fancy and chaotic creativity as a poet and artist. I love you both without end.

I hope these words inspire you, or make you think.
Above all, I want it to make you feel.

Contents

Part One

Part Two

Part One

Sing To me

Sing to me
A sweet lullaby
Crooning till the sweet late night
You look at me
And I dream away
Dreams still stand by to keep me sane

A heedless little dream of you
Lost in midnights twine we two
Drunken with our sweet desires
Lost inside a glance
Propels forbidden fire

Wake me when weaving your dream is done
To never touch the morning sun
Waiting till the day is done

You weave the spell of my dreams

Tidal

Your eyes
Control the rushing
Of my heart
The way the
Moon
Makes the tides
Wax and wane
To grow bigger
And stronger
Then to become
Weaker again

Sand

Under the beautiful moist sky
Holding my hand
As grains of sand sift
Between our toes
I counted it:
1
2
3
4
5
Times you said
"I love you"
In that many seconds
Too eager to prove
What only action
Could facilitate
Empty words
Invite broken promises

Ribbons and Twine

Wrap me in ribbons
And twine my friend
I need you like arms
To bind

So I won't fly away
So far my friend
To leave you
Far behind

All the prayers
And the wishes
You send my friend
Are sent now
All in vain

With ribbons and twine
I'll make wings
My friend
And leave you
All the same

Dangerous Lips and Fleeting Heart

I am an unsteady tide
> In turbulent waters

A branch of a fig tree
> Leaving fruit overly ripe

I am a lost idea
> In a mountain of considerations

A touch
> A substance

Liquid through your fingers
> I am a fleeting lust

Raised to a fever pitch
> A dream made to explore

But waking too soon
> I am an open book

With no typing on its pages
> Left for a reader's confusion

Sleep

Nothing to do
Nowhere to go
Life is on strings
Times going too slow

Another year older
Regrets are chin deep
Waste is lost time

Loves ravenous sleep

Remembering You

Stumbling through
The sweet and thunderous
Light of the evening

Cascading droplets
Of what feels like
Tears of the moon
Sounds of a gentle evening fall

Love

Distraction

When I see your face
The room is quiet
And your eyes focus on me

When I see your face
My words become broken
And I seem to lose my place

When I am in your presence
I stop my motion
And my longing seems to cease

Your intensity, uniqueness and insanity
Makes my mind spin
My heart begins to race

You throw me into distraction
This strange attraction
Will be my ending place

Angel on a cloud

Adoring and yearning

Eyes always on the vast and endless sea

Catching my breath

Not believing falling for you required this much

Heart languishing

In spite of itself

You

Fit the niche

Speak the language

Wear the garb

I only wait

To capture your breath

To feel your touch

As you confuse the mind

Of my Angel on a cloud

Soul to Body

My body is my home
My body is my house
My body I live in alone
Without a maid or spouse

Seek

Tis a pity walking alone
Tis a pity wandering on
Tis a pity never knowing
What it would be like to be with you

Is a night alone
Is a heart beating on
Is a tear not knowing
What it would be like to be with you

Floating very far
Dwelling with the stars
In my dreams you are
Wondering what it would be like to be with me

Quiet as you are
You couldn't be that far
You are always in my heart
That's beating rapidly

As my feelings change
You will still remain

A question still not changed is
Wondering what it would be like to be with you

Pour Me

Pour me
Like a glass of wine
Into your arms
I shall willingly go
My fluidity is yours

Gaze Upon you

So if I stare at you
Never mind
I only admire the hunger inside
Dreams that lie twitching
And ready to fly
I can see them all in your eyes

Jumping and writhing
Displaying emotion
Touching and crying
Decisive devotion
Enigmatically alluring
Pleasingly emotive
Strangely arousing
Yet mission devoted
And ever so physically pleasing, it's true

That's why my eyes forever gaze upon you

Ardent

Dark pools of passion I see in your eyes

I swim in them

Drown in them

The fool that is I

Can I ever take a living moment

Without a thought

A never ending lust for you?

As I bite my lip

It bleeds

I injured what I so long for you to kiss

Are passions alike?

Not one is like the other

Plain words

From injured lips

And aching heart

Fearing

It would be beyond my right to discover

Only

You are the only one
Who I have let quench my thirst
Has explored the hills and valleys
Of pleasure absent
As I am quickly speaking of denial
All you hear are words of lust
Whispering in your ear
Pretending I am already there
To make you follow suit
All I do is shake it off
And dream of another
Who will fill the rest of my night
With sweet surrender

Hidden Behind

How was I to know
When we first met
Just what my aversion
Would turn into
Dwelling in my head
As I sit on a concrete floor
Many times have my fingers drawn
At the corners of your smile
Imagining where your life will lead you
You are tucked away from me
Hidden behind
Cleaver retorts
And penetrating eyes

Cautious Curiosity

I have often wondered how you feel about me

My passion for you is indescribable

And sometimes confusing

Will I ever see you as I had seen you before

Could we meet

A salty deliciousness tickled by my tongue skin

By only fantasy

One of these days

I will see you

And when I do

I am going to look very closely

For a sign

So if I see it

I just might rush to tell you my feelings

Though not in words

For words could not describe

Be it a lust

Or a love for a different future

I will

Look into your eyes

Touch your arm

Kiss you

Like only a love of your vibes could

I want to be

Irresistible to you

So you cannot refuse

I have seen you look at me

And it excites me

One whole orgasmic feeling

Enveloped in an email

I do not dare send

Was I Just Another Face?

Was I just another face
Or was I something more?
Am I trying to reclaim
What my heart once lost before

Did you even take to me
The way I took to you
All you really know of me
Is what craziness comes through

Did you even care
Or did you even know
How much I do admire you
But tried not to let it show

For I sit here knowing
It's not a simple crush
It hurts me, just the thought of you
I'm dreaming way too much

I have never felt so strongly
About someone who's not mine

It comes out all so strangely
These twisted feelings I find

I know our hearts and minds

Are directed different ways

If only you knew the dreams of you

That fills my night and days

My feelings at this point

Don't matter very much

They will hide behind the smile I give
While waiting on your touch

Ache

I ache
To taste the lemon fill
And cup of tea
To lose my fingers
In the tangles of your hair
To smell the scent upon your clothes
Trace your lips lined in whiskey
To get butterflies in my stomach
I wait for you at your door
Disillusioned
Before you answer the call
The mood had passed
So I stumbled on unnoticed

My Heart

Soft as a newly bathed kitten

Blind as a love my heart beats out for you

Dangerous as the venom of an unbridled snake

Cold as a night alone in the dark

Lonely as the sun setting

Without the moon to meet him

And to never meet again

Reading into Things

Documents ridden with remnants of her

She's said it's a perfect suit of lies you've refined

Fingering the button holes down the front of your tailored jacket

Biting my tongue

Closing my eyes

Sinking my nails into my clammy palms

Breaking out into a cold sweat

Shaking my head

Dealing with my immaturity at length yet again

It Hurts when I Breathe

It hurts when I breathe
When I take in your air
It hurts to just be
When I only begin

I am down as you
I am down as well
Do I keep you down
Keep you from flying

I would leave a thousand miles away
Just to take away the pain
Do you remember playing chase
While being lost
In the darkness of our lives

Tears never drown the pain
When it hurts just to be you
The never complete

The only way to find yourself is on your own
Hoping to find some comfort in each other

Only developed into sandy ground

Silent words continue to be spoken

While the shadows move in the night

Your breath falls heavy

As we walk away forever

Junkie Love Song

Beautiful words you have spoken

To bring me out of my haze

I listen intently awaiting your smile

My diversion turned over a sharp corner

I am no better

I was cut so deeply

Not even you could breathe life into me again

I had cowered inside

Tried to crawl away

As you'd gotten

The best of me

Yet again

I wish I could go back and change

So that very moment will not exist

This stabbing pain now in my heart

Has chased away any chance of redemption

Socrates follows me to my grave

You affected me more than I imagined you could

Please leave me alone in my misery

Which until that moment ran deep and undisturbed

The Light Within

When I look at you
I see myself
The dark tipped with light
I want to touch the love
You're afraid to show
To let you in
To let you know
I see you
For who you cry out to be
But won't let anyone see
Saddened heart
Conscious mind
My heart cries out for more
The light within
Dark saddened heart
Afraid of being hurt
Loneliness is hard to bear
I want to comfort
I see you there
What you'll never know is
We are kindred hearts in our desires
I want to peel down the layers of you
And lie underneath
All the while
Feeling guilty
As I wander in this dream

Chewing on Leather

Consume me
Consummate me
Ask what you will

I have no lies
If you want me still

Taste it
Want it
Make me need
I want to be the authentic me

Feed on it
Fuel it
Find any excuse you can
Sin can make you a better man

Take no rest
Press softness against skin
To have a cheap grope
Might not be offensive

Take me down faster
You're taking forever
It's not my time yet
I'm chewing on leather

Every Aching Hour

Nothing can be said

Nothing can be heard

We cross boundaries

That led us to fault

It remains in our mind

Only to think in the backs of our heads

That it won't have a chance

We could never be together

So why did we start?

Start to love...

Start to haunt my thoughts and memories

Every aching hour

I could not leave though

So please don't you leave

I couldn't bear to never see you again

Even if you have read my poetry

Did you know it might have been you

I was writing about

I know nothing of you

Only what sweet glimpses

Of what you show me

What should I do?

As I start crooked

Only wanting to be straight with myself

Wanton Annoying

Blue

Green

Purple

And pink

Do you know how often I think?

Of how your body moves around

 My lips just pursing

Not making a sound

The look that crosses your curious eyes

That stares at me at a midnight high

I find myself only saying one thing

I feel queasy, where's the restroom?

Brave my Heart

I steadily move on foot by foot
I look on undisturbed
I lay there feeling lost
Looking for an answer
Maybe you might bestow on me
You make life interesting
You make life livable
Brave my Heart becomes
When I search for an answer
Every time I search
For comfort
For one who understands
I start at the beginning

To Serendipity

When first I met you, at the place
Where we both had worked
Thought nothing of the time
Thought nothing of it's worth

Sometimes people come to you
For teaching you a lesson
Sometimes they leave so quickly
You don't know what you're missin'

So thank you for your short time here
It will be remembered
You are a soul I'll truly miss
Of whom I'd say were kindred

Never Ending

Talk to another
You're talking in riddles
Unnerving accounts
Of a past unrelenting

Never ending

Gnaw through your bondage
Your leather straps
'Lost' is the word
Imprinted on them

Never ending

You live in a volunteer slavery
Liberate
Reincarnate
You would do anything

Never ending

Resist your craving
Push your own buttons
Before anyone can push them
You can't feel it where you're at
Even though it's there

So you search

Never ending

Dividing the risk
You give orders
Unfamiliar
Alien
Find it in your personal experience
Or in a subject only discussed by us

Never Satisfied

A page right out of your life

Exploring the wondering oasis
Driven into a black state of mind
Driving away
Alone as I wreak havoc on what is left of me

What I want
What is untouchable
What God forbids
What I forbid
I go on wanting anyway

I beg the shadows to bleed
The dark to saunter across me slowly
I invite its ruin
As I lay bare skinned
Wanton as flies to rotting meat

What Shall I Do?

Tapping me from behind
On my shoulder so slightly
Whispering softly
In my ear nightly
Dreams fly through my head
Frightening me
Touching my heart
Strikes me
So what shall I do now?

Eternal

Through my flesh

Through my blood

I pledge eternal love

Through the bright

Shining light

To the darkest blackest blight

Trust in me

And we will be

Together

Eternally

I Will Not Soon Forget You

It's very hard
To refuse to love you
I promised though
I would

You'll never know my eyes betrayed you
I never knew that one could

Though my heart lay right beside you
In the scariest of nights
Your brightness will
Subside till
I find another light

You are beautiful and tall
A man of whom I dream
My heart could cast
A thousand words
That my mind
Has pictured thee

For I might fall away
Far out of your blessed reach
Your tenderness and kind
Will be touched
And refuse to breach

You are a quiet soul

Of whom my thoughts belong

I will not soon forget you

Oh beautiful and strong

Another Take

Roses are Red

Violets are Blue

Love is a potion

I'll give to you

Memories are deep

Time has lost days

Healing will come

Come be what may

A Work Of Art

Your lips are like peach blossoms
Your eyes like precious jewels
Your hands like silken cloth
Your mind a clever tool
Your peace of mind like no other
Your strength will be at heart
Your love I will treasure always
      For it is a work of art

Down Dog

Yes
Right there
Your eyes so clear
Stare into the camera
Heart pulsing
All my breath
Taken for a whirl
On your yoga mat

Sometimes I Wish You Would Again

Sometimes I wish you would again

To take me in your arms again
I left you with a hell inside again
When all I wanted was to hide again

You are the light I tried to block again
When I was scared and shocked again
Why did I push you away again
Letting others rule and betray again

Now I will die every day again
Knowing I gave you away again
Now you'll never know
Before I let you go
Again

Rash Remiss

What was I thinking

When you came upon my step

To throw my life

And dreams up high

For a love I barely met

Running from my demons

Created even more

Chasing down a long lost dream

I lost so long before

Trying to reclaim

All my heart has desired

Will I reach my goal

Before time has expired

Dark as Wind Blows

Too hard the petal flows
Dark as wind blows
Oh how the stamp of a fiery steed
Gets fast indeed
Forever does my heart embrace
The world passing
Without grace
As
Your love will shatter
Life will scatter
Without the likes of me

Deceive Me

I ask you only one wish
And that is to deceive me
Please don't keep my heart in mind
You have no chance to believe me
In the house up on the hill
Or in my shadows dark and still
Love me not
Care for nothing
For I ask you only one wish
And that is to deceive me

Lost

This is all a big game for you isn't it

Looking down at me like I can be controlled

You know you have in the past

Had a huge hold on me

I cannot do

Or say

Or live

This way

Or take my own life

I am drowning

And feeling my veins boil

With anger

No love

No words

Have I

I'm lost
Again

Not Knowing What to Do Yet

Anonymous face

Do you see me

Really see me

Am I just making faces in the dark

Drawing life

With colored hair dye

In shades of blue

I am missing

I am missing pieces

I have pieces missing

Love all...

For whom?

Outsider

How could I be right
When my minds not in its place
I'm ashamed of what you've taught me
That rendered complete disgrace
If only I could avoid your world
If I am so inclined
I am such a lonely soul
And your company once divine
I wanted to fit in with you so badly
Now I am treated like an outsider
But more so madly

One Day without Rain

If your words are lies
When will your mischief end
You speak wildly
As your eyes grow dim
Another sign I get
As you turn your face
Another time I guess
Where your intentions misplace

And all I want
Is one day without rain
As bad as this drowning gets
I cannot complain
Just hold still while I speak my peace
Forgetting that night
To put my soul at ease

Listening to you
One heart beat away
Your tears are coming

Your making me pay
A cruel web we weave
When things you say complicate

And all I want

Is one day without rain

As bad as this drowning gets

I cannot complain

Just hold still while I speak my peace

Forgetting that night

To put my soul at ease

Never Say Forever

Never say forever
If you have no heart to give
Your words are quick and clever
You contort me like a sieve
You twist me inside out
And hung me up to dry
You waited for my downfall
And turned to say goodbye
Never say I love you
If you never really cared
Never show your feelings
If they were never really there
Never hold my hand
If you're going to break my heart
Never say you love me
If you never plan to start
Nothing lasts forever
I have not much to give
But if you truly love me
I might just let you in

To Replace or not to Replace

Why do I keep on searching
Constantly searching
For someone to take your place
Maybe to that trip across the lake
Maybe to that amusement park
That we carefully leave after dark
Or from the local show
To the occasional flow
Why do I want to replace you so

Another Girls Paradise

You are another girl's paradise
And another ones play toy
You're not of what she understands
The sweet perfection you are to me

Who can love you
And still be standing
It all comes down to my despair in the night
Of being alone without you
Forever

What I wouldn't do to touch you again
To love you fully and thoroughly
Knowing well in advance
I feel love for you
And it's just close friendship
You feel for me

I would gladly go back on my word to myself
The one that hurt so terribly
That I tried to convey to you

On a badly worded Saturday night
I have to block out the sights and sounds
Of someone you have loved and waited for
You will keep going back to her

Again and again

Now I'm dealing with the fact

I need you so much

And that someone you deeply love

Is in fact

Not me

I Was Made Invisible by You

I was made invisible to you

By thought of fear

You look right through me

A body smooth and clear

My mouth with no audible sound

My blood like water

Swimming around and around

I tell you how I feel

You don't hear me

I'm standing right here

You don't see me

I'm a thought

Not really there

I was made invisible by you

Home

You fall into pieces

You crawl in a hole

You need for salvation

The one you call home

Still wanting

Still wondering

Still in your mind

Yet in a moment of violent thought

As you struggle to conquer

Those demons within

Memories are so sharp

They left you bleeding

As you long for another human heart

Just as you fear it

For all you hear are good words

Laced with bad intentions

With apologies made

Not bought

For the price

Too costly

Always wondering

If you could ever fully love

Or trust again

Thoughts of a Broke Pyromaniac

My mind is going broke
Without a cent to spare
My memories have passed me by
Leaving nothing left to share
I want to lend my time and love
Where it is needed most
But time is of the essence
And my love is up in smoke

Everything

I lay myself down
My head under the moon
The night grows stiller yet
No matter how close we are
Not a move
Not a twitch

As I roll over to fondle
Slowly stirring
The simmering hungry
That is longing to escape

It hurts just the thought
Of knowing that
I won't always be
Your everything

Reflected Severance

We came as two

But now I fall

As you fade away

I was one

Now I'm gone

A wretched game to play

Reflected I came

Now alone

The day has lost its sheen

For now times lost

Now times drawn

It's last and living

Breath doth scream

Late Wisdom

I know you well

I knew you well

I told you things

I cannot tell

I fell in love

I fell on top

I saw the world

It meant a lot

I'm on the edge

I can't think straight

I used to love you

I learned too late

Dirty

There goes a piece of me
Flung out the window
Right into a mud puddle
Splashes on my outside
Dirty now like I am on the inside
Dirty now like the secret I am
I never liked a clean joke anyway

Part Two

Mechanics of my Mind

Am I imagining this
My mind sleeps perpetually
Boundaries fuzzy
Memories take place in the
Present tense

Last night's occurrences
Change their course in a deep slumber
To distinguish each day
Is almost always
Indistinguishable

Living while I'm awake
Living with my eyes closed
Vivid situations
Thrive within my tired mind

Sleepless darkness
Restless sheets
Groggy alertness
Attentive emotions
Spinning out of control
Spinning in and out of reality

Depression fades
Synthetic happiness numbs and tingles
Every inch
Depression recedes
Drugged calmness fails to perform any function.
Depression returns

I am here or am I somewhere else
I can't tell
Dreams dictate the mechanics of my mind

Broken

Dr. Mutilation
Taking my sanity
Along with my
Flawed
Machine of childbearing
With the stroke of his blade

To Be A Cat

Sometimes I wish
I were a cat
To purr dream deep
And all of that

Turn and flip
To chase the string
Eating tuna
Is just the thing

Yet I am human
A mere 5'4
Yet to be a cat
To stay indoors

I'd purr and sleep
And play all day
Never a worry
Comes to prey

Lay on the sill
Drink in the sun
And let my human
Rub my tum

Interests of people
Need not apply
Be not of human
Worries would I

Devils Repayment

You feel like hell

When you don't know

Where you come from

Stating an Angel completes a heart

That was wrapped inside a soul

That had viciously been torn

By all the tears you've shed

Make believe

Turn inside outside

Mind of warped thoughts

And you feel like the Devil

Who brings desires to you

Being the only feeling that is real

Not daring

To launch any questions of love

From your heart

Does she complete your heart

That was foiled by a soul

That was owed

To the Devil

For repayment

Ants

Ant,

Oh Ant,

How small you are

Red

Or green

Or black like tar

In your little hill

With a half a million cousins

Waiting for your bigamous wife to come

Are we lucky to

Crunch

Munch

Munch

On those of such

Chocolate covered

Served for lunch

In a dainty serving dish

Lip smacking

Sweetly covering my lips

YUCK!

I must be crazy to want to try to clamp

My hands on a can of chocolate-covered Ants

So don't ask me why

'Cos that is something I cannot answer

But I think

For now

I'll just stick to those plain unsalted nuts from planters.

Drag

My arms wrapped around him

As we rode on his motorcycle

He wore a beat up old leather jacket

I could feel all the cracks and pieces

Where the leather was torn and peeling

As I lean closer as not to fall

I could smell the addictions on his skin

Not a word escaped our lips

Even if there was a wanting to

As miles we go in search of peace and freedom

Winter Tale

Many days ago
In a weekend
In the month of January
Coldness wrought across the field
The wind is on the valley
Pain was on the frontier
Sweat in rivers flowed
Out onto the prairie
Where the hillsides grow
When the ground was thawed
Spring began to peep
Up through the lifeless branches
The trees began to leaf
As I sit there quietly
The wind whispered a tune
"You may think winter is over
But the breath of frost is soon"

March Rain

Rain Falls

Tiny floods

Where beetles crawl

Pill bugs

Curl upon themselves

Seeking shelter

Under the lemon balm

Time for bed

Taking my time going

Into slumber

Sock covered feet

A worn desk chair

A bed undone

And welcoming

So soft

Sheets

So cold

Waiting for my warm

Body

To wrap cotton sheaths

Over my skin

Time to rise

From the

Wooden and leather cradle

To accept a

Night devoid of flowering ideas

Tiny Vampire

Skeeter in my writing room

Munchin' on my finger

Drawing blood

Phlebotomist

Blood type O

Kismet

Hold the gun to my head

For you hold the game

Russian roulette

Pull the trigger

Sealed with a dry kiss

An eyeliner smudge

A drop of blood

Your bullet shattering infinite mirrors

Holding only the reflection of you

You can't hear my scream

Through all this cotton wool

And I can't see for blackness

The Beast

The beast inside
The bitch within
With little wings
Is rich and thin

Gemini Mind

All that I am
No one else is to blame
The same roots
Covered
With the soil of you

I am so much stunted
As I am a growth

Twins in the sky
Blamed for every bit
Of what my psychosis is

Orion needs to run

Equine

Galloping

Riding

Sprinting

Across the field

Steady as she goes

With one purpose

The freedom

The wind

The solemn nature

Oneness with the earth

Intrinsic

Spirited

At-the-ready

Powerful musculature

Under glistening coat

Regal in stature

Forever poised

For the ride

Dark Clouds

For there is not a sight of fair weather

So therefore no friends

Catching Fireflies

Star gazer
> You

Midnight rider
> Bathed

In twilight splendor
> Catching fireflies in the black sky

Held in
  Clear jars grasped with cold hands

I AM

Coward I am
Be still I am
Restrained I am
Too lame I am
Today I am
Wrong way I am
Be still I am
No thrill I am
Which way I am
Lost stray I am
Fog stayed I am
Not brave I am

Stained

Twisting foot
Walking up
Metal stairs
Hiding from
What demons
Take human form
Scared like a rabbit
Being hunted by dogs
With red stained skin
Where cruelty strikes

I Am Only Myself

I shall see always see

Dark

Never light

Disease travels through

Thy night

Female and male of kind

Shunning me

Breaking my mind

The hell has taken me

By night

Cold

Dark

Never light

They shall never help me

With my strife

I am hurting

Why?

For I am only myself

Watch Time Fly

Time oh time
What a monotonous game
The more you play
The less you gain

When procrastination
Sets the rules
You never win
You always lose

Wish

Straight hair is what I want

Never ending wishes

I think I am always just a dreamer
As I watch myself in the mirror
Wishing what could have been
As I wipe my carefully applied make-up
Torn down by a ribbon of tears

Old Shoes

She says "It has been a long time since we have spoken, what are you up to?"

Graciously declining all the new news

Tired of the new pumps

So I slip on the old shoes

I Doubt

Should I doubt my sunny sky

Thinking it is only a bright image

Covering the dark secrets in disguise

Should I doubt my land

So fertile and green

Pastures a many

Grains small but plenty

Should I shout to you

That the weather cast is rainy

And if you're not careful you'll drown

Or do I speak of what you know already

Surely heading death bound

I shout to you

For I doubt the ewe

That gives her milk to feed

I've tasted wine

Red cold wine

Like your blood I have received

In Me

Losing identity

Slipping from the edge of reality

You're watching

Waiting for me to fall

There was a pool of life

In me

That once rose high

Now water just collects

At the cracks

At the bottom

In disrepair

Immaculate Deception

To no manor born

Belonging to no man

Flimsy plastic pieces

Of someone else's plans

Nothing to subside on

Not even a single peep

So I go where the new tree grows

Cover my eyes and weep

When the night falls on

I go to white washed halls

Hang a silver lantern

On someone else's walls

Speak a gentle lullaby

And a prayer or two

Kiss my doll to sleep

And lay in bed till noon

Get up and surprised to find

That I've become deaf and blind

Feeling that my speech meant nothing...

I suppose I have nothing left to say

Mustard and Honey

Bee spit

Cracked peppercorn

Crunchy runny

Goes down the gullet well

Would our spit be like honey

To a larger life form

If we sucked on pollen from flowers and regurgitated it?

"Pardon me; do you have any Grey Poupon?"

The Last Night the Last Day

The last night
The last day
I heard from you
Was one I shall forget
You'll never know
Why I hate you
I wished we'd never met

You drug me through
Beneath the grave
Of my past put to rest
And hoped to bring back
Tears and hate
Brought about by my grandmothers death

The last night
The last day
I had hoped to see you here
Was the day before I matured to womanhood
Concluded the last several years

I mean this with a passion
Only fire could forsake

With a true bred animosity
Hatred by my blade

The last night
The last day
I ever saw you here
Was in the attic
Tiptoeing
Through the wall then disappeared

You heard me
Saw me cry out to
And plead you go away
No reason you have being here
But still you won't obey

The last night
The last day
You will leave me be
Is when I'm on my death bed

And soon to follow thee

To that place I'll go
Where you'll be waiting there
Hand in hand with Orion
And to the Lord I'd swear
The last night
The last day
That I will roam this house
Is when you are on your death bed
And take my place

Tiptoeing through the house

The Grapes of Wrath

The grapes of wrath

Proceeds to be

Hanging there in its luxury

With vines that twine around my wrist

That you have put there just for this

So you can mock at the sight

So the grapes of wrath

I taste for you tonight

Filthy

Pick up and leave

Whenever I panic
Fight or flight
When alone
My mind
A strange bedfellow
She tells me I'm filthy
I believe her
Why would she lie
She's my mother

Dead Forgotten

Careful

Creeping

Dark

And

Still

Death is close

So write your will

Leave me nothing

But yet remember

You

Are

No longer

My family member

Through Drawn and Betrayal

Though I dread to see it
I am somehow drawn to it
Through eyes that have often betrayed me

I have come to detest my dreaded mind
To the point of disillusion
The place that I've been raised
And planted to grow
As THEY want
The seed of my life
Was forced into this
To strive on
To be no one
The water and feed to flourish
My green and growing leaves
I did not take
Afraid to take
In case of poisoning

I shall grow alone
Away from the place I've been

Though I dread to see it
I am somehow drawn to it
Through the eyes
That have often betrayed me

It's Been a Long Time

It's been a long time my friend
Of my pencil and pen
Not once did I hear my paper calling me
I guess it must have given up
From then on to the count of three

I didn't hear it calling me

Do you love me as I love you?
Just one dependence this is true
Paper cannot love a pen
So I guess I am no different than

It's true I've missed you, my dear friend
The only one that hears my little tales
Left untold to human ears

Oh dear friend
I promise you now

That I was gone then
But I'm not gone now

More

"Just a little bit more" I said as I pushed the last French fry down.

'I can work it off later' I thought to myself as a pretty young thing passed me at the dinner table.

Her skin was perfect.

Her figure delicately framed.

Looking down, viewing her through my eyelashes, guilt crossed me like a burial shroud.

"Would you like a slice of cherry pie, it was freshly made?" The thin girl said softly.

I just looked up at her, shook my head, crossed the room and ran away.

In the Glow of the Forest

In the glow of the forest
In the shadows of the trees
I will fear no more
For when evil comes
By the black cold fog
I will fight to the death
Alone and tall
Until one survives through it all
I will stab
I will cut
I will hit
Through the gut
Of the wretched cold mangled leaves
This demon of fear
Will settle it here
Then I will rise out of the dark

The Simple Truth

What mud is this?

I'd ask, I'd hear

I thought I put a nickel here

Maybe a dime

A quarter at most

What drink is this?

I'll make a toast

What song is this?

I've heard it before

Yes, the one about peace and love

Not war

Let's dance to it

Sing along in scores

Frolic and play

Be happy and more

Life is this

 I know it well

But some go to heaven

And some go to hell

Behind Enemy Lines

Secrets touching me like a razor in its anger

Behold me or Hold me

Like I'm some foul disease

Lithe feelings

Playing your guilt

Like a red rose ready to wilt

I flinch at your voice

And this contort of my heart

I know too well

Of this story

So I stop and stay placid

As you wish me to be

You talk about "I"

Although I'll spill

My mind recklessly

So follow my thoughts

Be they ragged or smooth

Follow your way

Or escape to my doom

Your tongue will be tied

Yield your heart and forget your mind

You're cut by the razor

You anxiously gave

So bleed on forever

And don't be afraid

You're only a memory that I once forgave

How I wish you weren't

A diabolical slave

Boundless

Lead the way

Dare

Follow the path

That

Leads to who you are

"For I know the plans I have for you"

Says he

We are all made unique

Don't be afraid of

Who you are

No bounds to the soul

When you go with what your heart needs

Feel at peace, rest your mind, get that dream!

4 Days till Friday

4 days till Friday
I cannot wait
4 days till Friday
I hope I won't be late

4 days till Friday
Soon to come
4 days till Friday
For Monday is done

Why wait
Anticipate
The week's mighty end

To finish it off
And start all over again

A Brave but Bitter End

He played

He lost

His death is to come

He tried and wrought his fingers numb

He worked through dusk

And more through dawn

His blood grows still

His death forsworn

He'll grow weaker

Till he knows his work is nothing

For nothing is shown

He sells his soul,

And has what to show?

Life set adrift

Blown away

Never had I seen

A man so brave

An artistic person by nature, Megan has a background in stage acting, music, painting, sculpture, photography, and graphic design. She is a powerhouse of artistry and presentation. Megan has been creating poetry since she was a child and is in love with the poetic art form. She lives in Northern California with her husband, daughter, and her many recued animals.

https://www.facebook.com/geekgirlwho

https://twitter.com/MeganBenEvans

http://instagram.com/geekgirlwho

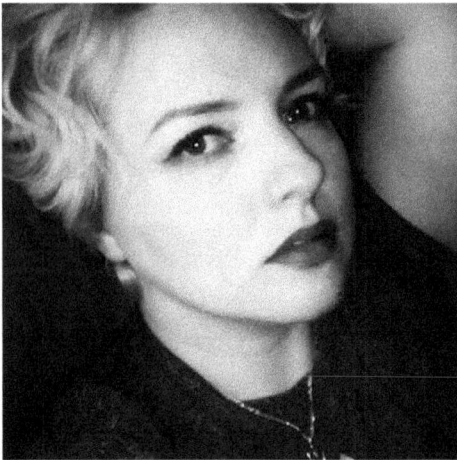

www.ingramcontent.com/pod-product-compliance
Lightning Source LLC
Chambersburg PA
CBHW070813050426
42452CB00011B/2019